Hello, my name is Jeremy Tubbs, and I invite you to join me on a journey to explore the sons of Judah—figures whose influence extends far beyond the pages of ancient scripture. As we dive into their stories, we will uncover their roles in the biblical narrative, their complex legacies, and the significance of their bloodline.

Through the stories of Er, Onan, Shelah, Perez, and Zerah, we will explore timeless themes of faith, morality, redemption, and divine purpose. These figures, often seen as distant ancestors, continue to hold relevance in today's world, offering insights into identity, spirituality, and the ways in which history shapes our present.

I encourage you to dive deep with me into these narratives, to reflect on their meanings, and to uncover how the legacy of the sons of Judah speaks to us today. Together, let's uncover the profound connections between the past and the present, and illuminate the powerful truths within these ancient stories.

As we explore the sons of Judah, we'll see that their story is more than just a historical account—it's a mirror to the challenges and triumphs that define human existence. The choices they made, the trials they faced, and the blessings they received hold deep lessons for us today. Whether it's the tale of Judah's own struggle with integrity, the moral complexities surrounding his sons, or the enduring legacy of their descendants, there's much to uncover.

Each son, in his own way, reflects broader themes of lineage, justice, redemption, and faith. Through their stories, we gain a clearer understanding of how personal actions can shape the course of history and how divine purposes are often revealed through human choices.

I invite you to look beyond the surface, to engage with these ancient figures not just as characters from the past, but as enduring symbols whose lessons still speak to us today. Let's explore how the bloodline of Judah continues to influence our world and what these stories can teach us about

our own journeys.

The Tribe of Judah is one of the twelve tribes of

Israel, named after Judah, the fourth son of Jacob

(also known as Israel) and Leah. In the Bible,

Judah stands out for his significant role in both the

history of Israel and in biblical prophecy. The Tribe

of Judah is often associated with leadership,

strength, and the fulfillment of God's promises.

In Genesis 49, when Jacob blesses his sons,

Judah receives a special blessing. Jacob

prophesies that Judah will be the leader of his

brothers, saying, *"The scepter will not depart from*

Judah, nor the ruler's staff from between his feet..."

(Genesis 49:10). This prophetic statement points to the future leadership of the tribe, with the ultimate fulfillment in the kingship of David and the lineage of Jesus Christ, who, according to the New Testament, is from the Tribe of Judah.

The Bible also highlights Judah's role in the formation of the Israelite nation. After the Israelites leave Egypt, it is the Tribe of Judah that is often at the forefront of military campaigns and leadership. For example, in the book of Numbers, Judah is described as leading the way when the Israelites march through the wilderness (Numbers 2:3-9).

The Tribe of Judah is also distinguished for its association with the Davidic dynasty. King David,

Israel's most famous king, hailed from this tribe.

The Bible describes him as a man after God's own

heart, and it was through David's line that God

promised an eternal kingdom, which Christians

believe was fulfilled through Jesus Christ, the "Lion

of Judah."

The Tribe of Judah is central not only in the Old

Testament but also in the New Testament. Jesus is

frequently referred to as the "Lion of the Tribe of

Judah" (Revelation 5:5), emphasizing the

messianic connection to this tribe and its enduring

significance in God's plan of redemption.

In summary, the Tribe of Judah holds a place of

prominence in the Bible, both as a symbol of

leadership and as the line through which the Messiah would come. Its legacy is one of spiritual and royal authority, with roots deep in the history and prophecy of Israel.

The significance of the Tribe of Judah goes beyond its historical and prophetic roles. In addition to the royal lineage of David and the messianic promise, the tribe also holds a symbolic place in the broader narrative of the Bible. Judah's story begins with personal transformation and growth, particularly when we consider the early struggles of his character. For instance, Judah's actions early in the book of Genesis reflect a troubled past, including his involvement in the betrayal of his brother Joseph. Yet, his eventual willingness to sacrifice for his family, particularly in the story of his interaction with Joseph in Egypt (Genesis 44-45), shows profound personal growth and repentance.

Judah's change of heart and leadership qualities are reflected in the tribe that carries his name. The Tribe of Judah is noted for its strength and courage, as well as its deep connection to the promises God made to Israel. After the Israelites entered the Promised Land, it was the tribe of Judah that received the largest portion of land in the south of Israel, with its territory including the city of Jerusalem. This was significant, as

Jerusalem became the capital of Israel under King David's reign, and later, the site of the Temple.

Throughout the Bible, the Tribe of Judah is often seen as the tribe of kings. King David, and later his descendants, ruled Israel from this tribe. The importance of Judah's kingship is further emphasized in the prophecies of the coming Messiah. In Isaiah 11:1, it is prophesied that a "shoot will come up from the stump of Jesse," a reference to David's father, indicating that the Messiah would come from the royal lineage of Judah.

The Tribe of Judah also represents faithfulness to God's covenant. In the history of Israel, Judah's kings and leaders were called to remain faithful to God, and while some were unfaithful, others, like King Hezekiah and King Josiah, sought to bring spiritual renewal to Israel. Despite times of unfaithfulness, God's promises to Judah, including the promise of an everlasting kingdom, remain steadfast.

In the New Testament, the significance of Judah is clearly highlighted in the person of Jesus Christ. Jesus' birth in Bethlehem, in the land of Judah, and his Davidic lineage, fulfill the Old Testament prophecies. Jesus is seen as the ultimate fulfillment of the promise that the scepter would not depart from Judah, signifying not only His royal authority but His divine kingship as the Savior of the world.

Thus, the Tribe of Judah is not only a historical entity but a living symbol of leadership, redemption, and divine promise. From the ancient kingdom of Israel to the coming of the Messiah, Judah's legacy continues to shape the biblical story and provide hope and direction for believers today.

The bloodline of the Tribe of Judah is rich with significance, both in terms of its historical and spiritual legacy. This lineage represents the fulfillment of divine promises, particularly those of leadership, kingship, and the coming of the Messiah.

Judah's Descendants: A Royal Lineage

The bloodline of Judah begins with Judah himself, the fourth son of Jacob and Leah. While Judah's early life was marked by struggles and mistakes, his eventual leadership within the family of Jacob set the stage for the tribe's prominence. As mentioned earlier, in **Genesis 49:10**, Jacob prophesied that the scepter would not depart from Judah, signaling that this tribe would hold a position of leadership over Israel.

Judah's own descendants, most notably King David, represent the peak of the tribe's influence. David, a young shepherd from Judah, was anointed by God to become the king of Israel. His reign marked a significant period in Israel's history, and God made a covenant with David, promising that his descendants would rule over Israel forever (2 Samuel 7:16). This promise laid the foundation for the bloodline of Judah, which would eventually lead to the birth of Jesus Christ, the Messiah.

The Importance of the Davidic Line

The Davidic line is central to the understanding of Judah's bloodline. The Bible emphasizes that the Messiah would come from the lineage of David. This is repeatedly mentioned in both the Old and New Testaments. In **Isaiah 11:1**, the prophet foretold that the Messiah would come from the "stump of Jesse"—Jesse being the father of David.

This establishes the connection between Judah, David, and the coming of a savior who would bring redemption to Israel and the world.

In the New Testament, the genealogy of Jesus is presented in both the Gospels of Matthew and Luke. Matthew traces Jesus' lineage through David, emphasizing His descent from the Tribe of Judah. This connection underscores Jesus as the fulfillment of God's promises to Judah and David. **Matthew 1:1** begins the genealogy by stating, *"This is the genealogy of Jesus the Messiah, the son of David, the son of Abraham."* This establishes Jesus as a rightful heir to the promises made to both Abraham and David, highlighting His royal and spiritual significance.

The Legacy of Judah: From Kings to the Messiah

While the kingdom of Judah eventually fell to the Babylonians, the bloodline of Judah continued through the generations, even in times of exile. The descendants of Judah, though many were scattered or in captivity, continued to be a people marked by their covenant with God. Despite political upheavals and challenges, the bloodline of Judah remained central in God's plan for redemption.

The New Testament presents Jesus as the "Lion of the Tribe of Judah" (Revelation 5:5), signifying His connection to Judah's royal bloodline. Jesus, though born into humble circumstances, was fully recognized as the fulfillment of the Messianic prophecies. His bloodline, though seemingly ordinary, carried with it the eternal promise of salvation for all humanity.

The Spiritual Legacy of Judah's Bloodline

The bloodline of Judah is not just about physical descent but also carries spiritual significance. Throughout the Bible, God's faithfulness to Judah's descendants is a recurring theme. The tribe of Judah represents God's covenantal promise to His people, and through this bloodline, we see how divine purpose is carried out over generations.

The Apostle Paul, in his letters, especially in the book of Romans, emphasizes that those who are spiritually united with Christ become part of the "Israel of God" (Galatians 6:16). While the physical descendants of Judah remain significant, the New Testament teaches that the true bloodline of Judah extends beyond ethnicity to include all those who are united with Christ through faith.

Judah's Bloodline Today

The legacy of Judah's bloodline continues to influence not only the Jewish people but also Christians, who see themselves as grafted into the promises made to Israel. In this way, Judah's

descendants, both physical and spiritual, form a

bridge between the Old and New Testaments,

pointing to God's ultimate plan for redemption

through Jesus Christ.

Through the bloodline of Judah, we are reminded

of God's faithfulness, the importance of divine

promises, and the centrality of Christ in the story of

salvation. The legacy of Judah lives on in both

historical and spiritual terms, continuing to shape

the faith and hope of millions across the world.

The Israelites, the descendants of the twelve sons

of Jacob (whose name was later changed to

Israel), are central to the biblical narrative. They

represent God's chosen people, with a unique covenantal relationship with God that sets them apart from other nations. The story of the Israelites is one of divine promise, struggle, redemption, and fulfillment. Their journey, from slavery in Egypt to their establishment as a nation in the Promised Land, reflects the overarching themes of faith, obedience, and God's faithfulness.

The Birth of Israel

The foundation of the Israelite people begins with Jacob, who had twelve sons, each of whom would become the progenitor of one of the twelve tribes of Israel. These tribes, including Judah, were initially united as one family under Jacob. However, due to a series of events—most notably Joseph's sale into slavery by his brothers—the Israelites eventually found themselves in Egypt, where they were enslaved for several generations.

God's covenant with the patriarchs—Abraham, Isaac, and Jacob—was the defining promise that shaped the identity of the Israelites. God had promised Abraham that his descendants would become a great nation and that through them, all nations would be blessed (Genesis 12:3, 17:4-5). This promise was reaffirmed to Isaac and Jacob, marking the Israelites as God's chosen people.

The Exodus and the Covenant at Sinai

The story of the Israelites truly begins in earnest with their deliverance from slavery in Egypt, an event known as the Exodus. Under the leadership of Moses, God miraculously freed the Israelites from bondage, demonstrating His power and faithfulness. The Exodus was a pivotal moment in Israelite history, symbolizing both physical and spiritual liberation. It also marked the beginning of the Israelites' journey toward becoming a nation, with God as their sovereign ruler.

At Mount Sinai, God established a covenant with the Israelites, giving them the Law (including the Ten Commandments) and a set of guidelines for living as His holy people. This covenant was based on the idea that if the Israelites obeyed God, they would be blessed and protected, but if they disobeyed, they would face judgment. The Israelites' ability to follow God's commands was repeatedly tested throughout their journey, with varying degrees of faithfulness.

The Promised Land

After wandering in the wilderness for forty years, the Israelites, under the leadership of Joshua, entered the Promised Land, the land God had promised to give them. This conquest was not only a physical victory but also a spiritual one. The land was symbolic of God's faithfulness to His promises and was to be a place where the Israelites could worship Him freely and live according to His commands.

However, even after settling in the Promised Land, the Israelites struggled with idolatry, disobedience, and division. They went through cycles of sin and repentance, with periods of prosperity followed by times of oppression and defeat. The period of the judges, when Israel was led by various leaders raised up by God, is characterized by this instability.

The Establishment of the Kingdom

The Israelites eventually demanded a king, desiring to be like the other nations around them. Despite God's warning that having a human king would lead to oppression and idolatry, God allowed the Israelites to have a king. The first king of Israel was Saul, from the tribe of Benjamin, but it was David, from the Tribe of Judah, who became the most notable and beloved king of Israel.

Under King David, Israel was united as a powerful kingdom, and Jerusalem was established as its capital. God made a covenant with David, promising that his descendants would rule over Israel forever, setting the stage for the Messianic promise that Jesus, the descendant of David, would fulfill.

The Divided Kingdom

After Solomon, David's son, Israel experienced a

division. The northern ten tribes rebelled against

the southern kingdom of Judah, which was

composed of the tribes of Judah and Benjamin.

This split resulted in the creation of two separate

kingdoms: the Kingdom of Israel (the northern

kingdom) and the Kingdom of Judah (the southern

kingdom).

The Kingdom of Israel was eventually conquered

by the Assyrians in 722 BCE, and the ten tribes of

Israel were scattered, becoming known as the "Ten

Lost Tribes." The Kingdom of Judah, on the other

hand, continued for a longer period but was

eventually conquered by the Babylonians in 586

BCE. The destruction of Jerusalem and the exile of the people to Babylon marked a major turning point in Israelite history, signaling the end of the monarchy and the loss of the political independence the Israelites had enjoyed.

The Return and the Restoration

After seventy years of exile, the Israelites were allowed to return to their land under the Persian king Cyrus. This period of return was marked by the rebuilding of Jerusalem and the Temple, but the Israelites remained under foreign domination, first by the Persians, then the Greeks, and eventually the Romans.

Despite these external pressures, the Israelites maintained a distinct cultural and religious identity, with the worship of Yahweh (God) at the center of their lives. During this time, prophets like Isaiah, Jeremiah, and Ezekiel foretold of a coming Messiah who would restore the kingdom of Israel and bring peace and salvation to God's people.

The Spiritual Journey of the Israelites

The story of the Israelites is not just a historical account but a spiritual journey that reflects the broader human experience. The Israelites' relationship with God is marked by moments of deep faith and obedience as well as rebellion and spiritual failure. The recurring themes of covenant, redemption, and restoration are woven throughout their history.

Through the Israelites, God reveals His justice and mercy, showing that even in times of failure, there is always the hope of redemption through repentance and faith. The Israelites were called to be a light to the nations, a people who would reveal God's glory to the world. In the New Testament, Christians believe that Jesus, the Messiah, came not only to fulfill the promises made to Israel but also to extend God's salvation to all people, offering a way for everyone to be reconciled to God.

The Israelites and Their Legacy Today

Today, the legacy of the Israelites continues to shape the faith and beliefs of millions. Judaism, Christianity, and Islam all trace their spiritual roots back to the covenant God made with the Israelites. The story of the Israelites serves as both a foundation for these faiths and a profound lesson in God's faithfulness and grace. The journey of the Israelites, from slavery to freedom, from disobedience to redemption, reflects the ongoing spiritual journey of God's people, encouraging all believers to trust in His promises and remain faithful to His calling.

In today's times, identifying the descendants of the ancient Israelites—particularly those from the twelve tribes—can be complex, as centuries of dispersion, migration, and intermarriage have blurred the lines of direct lineage. However, there are still groups and communities that consider themselves descendants of the Israelites or have been traditionally associated with the biblical tribes. These groups can be classified in different ways based on religious, cultural, and ethnic identity.

1. The Jewish People:

The Jewish people are the most prominent group today who identify as descendants of the ancient Israelites. Modern Judaism traces its roots to the Kingdom of Judah, the southern kingdom after the division of Israel, and its capital, Jerusalem. This includes the descendants of the tribes of Judah,

Benjamin, and some of the Levites who were

involved in religious duties.

- **The Tribe of Judah:** As the largest and

  most influential tribe, many Jews today can

  trace their lineage back to the Tribe of

  Judah. This includes the royal line of King

  David, and, by Christian belief, Jesus Christ

  is also descended from this tribe. Jews of

  today who claim descent from the Tribe of

  Judah often identify as part of the larger

  Jewish community.

- **The Tribe of Benjamin:** Some Jewish

  families, especially those from certain

regions or traditions, claim descent from the Tribe of Benjamin, which was closely associated with Judah. The Apostle Paul, for example, famously identifies as a "Benjamite" in the New Testament (Romans 11:1).

- **The Levites:** The Levites, the tribe that provided priests and religious leaders for Israel, are another significant group in Jewish tradition. Today, many Jews who are descendants of the Levites carry the surname "Cohen" or "Kohan," which refers to their priestly lineage.

2. The Lost Ten Tribes:

The ten northern tribes of Israel, which were exiled by the Assyrians in 722 BCE, are often referred to as the "Ten Lost Tribes." These tribes are believed to have been dispersed across various regions, and their exact fate remains a mystery. Over time, numerous theories and traditions have developed about where these tribes might have gone, with some groups claiming to be descendants of these lost tribes.

- **The Samaritans:** One of the most well-known groups that claim descent from the northern tribes is the Samaritans. Historically, the Samaritans were closely related to the Israelites, but over time, they became distinct due to differences in

religious practice and worship. Today, there

is a small community of Samaritans living

primarily in Israel and the West Bank.

- **Modern Claims of Descent from the Lost Tribes:** Various ethnic groups around the world, including some in Africa, India, and the Americas, have claimed descent from the lost tribes of Israel. For instance, groups such as the Beta Israel (Ethiopian Jews), the Bnei Menashe (in India), and the Igbo (in Nigeria) have been proposed as descendants of these lost tribes, though these claims are often debated and researched.

3. The State of Israel:

In modern times, the establishment of the State of Israel in 1948 has brought together Jews from all over the world, many of whom are descendants of the ancient Israelites. The majority of Israelis are ethnically Jewish, with their ancestors tracing their roots to the ancient tribes of Israel. However, the identity of modern Israel as a nation-state is not solely based on tribal descent but on religious and cultural continuity.

4. Christians and the Spiritual Legacy:

In Christianity, the spiritual descendants of Israel are often seen as all believers in Christ, regardless of ethnic background. Christians believe that through faith in Jesus, they are grafted into the promises given to Israel, as Paul explains in Romans 11. This concept of being "spiritually" connected to Israel is key to understanding how Christianity views the modern descendants of Israel. For Christians, the Tribe of Judah is particularly significant as it is through this tribe that Jesus, the Messiah, was born.

5. The African Connection:

In Africa, there are several groups who claim or are believed to be descended from the Israelites, particularly those who are traditionally seen as part of the ancient diaspora. One well-known group is the **Ethiopian Jews (Beta Israel)**, who have lived in Ethiopia for centuries and have a long history of claiming descent from the tribe of Dan, one of the lost ten tribes. They immigrated to Israel in large numbers during the 1980s and 1990s as part of operations like **Operation Moses** and **Operation Solomon**.

6. Other Communities:

- **The Igbo People of Nigeria:** There have been claims, both from within the Igbo community and outside, that the Igbo people of Nigeria are descendants of the ancient

Israelites, specifically from the Tribe of Gad or the Tribe of Levi. This belief is part of a broader movement of African identity rooted in biblical traditions.

- **The Lemba People of Southern Africa:** The Lemba are a group of people in southern Africa who claim descent from Jewish ancestors, and they have certain cultural and religious practices that resemble Jewish customs, such as circumcision and dietary laws.

oday, the Israelites, in a direct ethnic and cultural sense, are primarily identified with the Jewish people. However, the term "Israelites" can take on different meanings depending on historical,

religious, and cultural contexts. Let's break this

down:

1. The Jewish People:

The primary descendants of the ancient Israelites

are the Jewish people. This includes those who

identify ethnically, culturally, and religiously with the

Jewish tradition, as well as those who are

descendants of the tribes of Israel.

- **Ethnic Jews:** The Jewish people today

  trace their ancestry back to the tribes of

  Israel, particularly the tribes of Judah,

  Benjamin, and Levi. The tribe of Judah is

  especially significant, as it produced the

kings of Israel, including King David, and

Jesus Christ (according to Christian belief).

Jews today are often seen as the direct

descendants of the Israelites in both a

physical and spiritual sense.

- **Modern Israel:** The State of Israel,

established in 1948, is home to millions of

Jewish people from around the world,

including those who trace their roots back to

the ancient Israelites. This includes Jews

who have emigrated from Europe, North

Africa, the Middle East, Ethiopia, and even

from communities in Asia and the Americas.

The population of Israel today represents a

modern continuation of the ancient Israelite identity, both through their Jewish religious heritage and their connection to the biblical land of Israel.

2. The Samaritans:

The Samaritans are another group that can be considered descendants of the ancient Israelites, specifically from the northern tribes. They trace their lineage back to the Israelites who remained in the land of Israel after the Assyrian conquest of the northern kingdom in 722 BCE. While they share many religious practices with Jews, such as the worship of the God of Israel and the observance of certain holy days, they have their own distinct identity and traditions. Today, there is a small

Samaritan community living in Israel and the West

Bank, specifically in the city of Nablus and the town

of Holon.

3. The Lost Tribes of Israel:

The Ten Lost Tribes refer to the northern kingdom

of Israel that was conquered by the Assyrians in

722 BCE. These tribes were scattered across

various regions and largely lost to history, with

many theories and claims about their fate. Some

believe that certain groups around the world,

particularly in Africa, India, and the Americas, are

descendants of these lost tribes, though these

claims are often debated and not universally accepted.

- **Beta Israel (Ethiopian Jews):** One group often associated with the lost tribes is the Beta Israel community in Ethiopia. Many Ethiopian Jews claim descent from the tribe of Dan, one of the ten lost tribes. This community was largely recognized as Jewish, and in the late 20th century, many Ethiopian Jews immigrated to Israel through operations like Operation Moses and Operation Solomon.

- **Bnei Menashe (India):** The Bnei Menashe, a group in northeastern India, claim descent from the tribe of Manasseh, one of the ten lost tribes. They have practiced Jewish customs and have sought recognition from Israel, some of whom have immigrated there in recent years.

- **The Igbo People (Nigeria):** There are claims that the Igbo people of Nigeria are descendants of the ancient Israelites, potentially from the tribe of Gad or other tribes. Some Igbo people practice traditions that resemble Jewish customs, such as circumcision and observing the Sabbath, though the connection to ancient Israel is not definitively established.

- **The Lemba (Southern Africa):** The Lemba people of Southern Africa also claim descent from Jews, specifically from the tribe of Levi. Genetic studies have shown some evidence of Jewish ancestry among the Lemba, suggesting a potential historical connection to the ancient Israelites.

4. Christianity and the Spiritual Israelites:

In Christian theology, the concept of the "Israelites" extends beyond ethnic descent. Christians believe that, through faith in Jesus Christ, Gentiles (non-Jews) are spiritually grafted into the promises made to Israel, becoming part of the "spiritual Israel." The Apostle Paul, in his letters (particularly in Romans 11), explains that Gentile believers in Christ are spiritually adopted into the covenant God made with Israel.

This idea has had a significant influence on Christian understanding, where believers are seen as part of the broader spiritual family of Israel, regardless of their ethnic heritage.

5. Messianic Jews:

There is also a movement within Christianity called **Messianic Judaism**, where Jews who believe in Jesus as the Messiah continue to identify as Israelites, combining Jewish heritage with the belief that Jesus fulfilled the messianic prophecies of the Hebrew Bible. These Jews view themselves as both ethnically Jewish and spiritually connected to the larger body of Israel through their faith in Jesus Christ.

In today's world, many people in America and beyond claim to be Israelites, but the challenge often arises when they don't follow the laws or commandments that were historically central to the identity of the Israelites. So, what are the rules that they should be following? Let me break it down for you.

1. The Ten Commandments (Exodus 20 and Deuteronomy 5):

The **Ten Commandments** are a fundamental starting point. These commandments were given to the Israelites by God through Moses, and they form

the moral backbone of the Israelite faith. They are

not just rules but principles that govern the

relationship between the people and God, as well

as how they treat each other. Here's a quick look at

them:

- **No other gods** besides Yahweh (the God of Israel).

- **No idols** or graven images.

- **Honor the Sabbath day** and keep it holy.

- **Honor your father and mother.**

- **No murder, adultery, theft, or false witness** against your neighbor.

- **Do not covet** what belongs to your neighbor.

These commandments emphasize that a true Israelite is expected to live with integrity, honor, and a deep commitment to worshiping and respecting God. They form the foundation of the moral law that should govern the lives of those who identify as Israelites.

2. The 613 Mitzvot (Commandments):

In addition to the Ten Commandments, the Torah contains **613 commandments**—called the **Mitzvot**—which cover nearly every aspect of life, from personal behavior to religious observance.

These laws are the blueprint for how an Israelite should live in both spiritual and everyday matters.

Here are some key areas that the Mitzvot address:

- **Worship and Sacrifices:** While the practice of animal sacrifices is no longer in effect since the destruction of the Second Temple, the spirit of proper worship is still essential. The Israelites were commanded to worship Yahweh exclusively and to approach their faith with reverence and devotion. Today, this translates into observing prayer, honoring the Sabbath, and dedicating time to study the Torah and live by its teachings.

- **Dietary Laws (Kashrut):** One of the more well-known aspects of the Mitzvot is the dietary laws, often referred to as **kosher** laws. These laws dictate what food is permissible (clean) and forbidden (unclean) for the Israelites to eat. For example, they are prohibited from eating pork or shellfish, and meat and dairy cannot be consumed together.

- **Social Justice and Fairness:** The Mitzvot also lay out principles of justice, including caring for the poor, the stranger, the widow, and the orphan. Israelites were commanded to act justly in all their dealings, and to be generous and fair in their treatment of others. This includes laws related to lending, business ethics, and the treatment of workers.

- **Holiness and Purity:** Many of the commandments focus on maintaining purity—whether moral, physical, or spiritual. This includes instructions on rituals of cleanliness, sexual ethics, and purity in religious practice. It calls for a life of holiness, reflecting the holiness of God.

3. The Festivals and Holy Days:

The Israelites were commanded to observe certain **festivals** and **holy days** throughout the year to commemorate key events in their history and relationship with God. Some of the most important ones include:

- **Passover (Pesach):** Celebrating the Israelites' liberation from slavery in Egypt.

- **Shavuot (Feast of Weeks):** Celebrating the giving of the Torah at Mount Sinai.

- **Sukkot (Feast of Tabernacles):** Commemorating the time the Israelites spent in the wilderness after leaving Egypt.

- **Yom Kippur (Day of Atonement):** A day of repentance and atonement for sins.

- **Rosh Hashanah (Jewish New Year):** A time of reflection and renewal.

These festivals help keep the memory of Israel's unique relationship with God alive and are meant to be times of worship, reflection, and celebration.

4. The Laws of Prayer and Worship:

For those who identify as Israelites, regular **prayer** and **worship** are key components of daily life. The Jewish prayer book, the **Siddur**, includes specific prayers to be recited daily, and synagogue worship is a central part of the Israelite tradition. Observing the Sabbath (Shabbat), from Friday evening to Saturday evening, is a sacred day of rest, prayer, and family time.

Let me share a story with you, one that paints a vivid picture of someone's journey into a new identity but still grappling with the complexities of life and the challenges of truly living out those beliefs.

Marcus grew up in the streets of the city. Raised in the chaos of gang violence, he was a Crip from the age of 12, drawn into the life by the need for protection, respect, and a sense of belonging. His days were spent trying to survive, making decisions that reflected his environment—where loyalty to the gang was paramount and the struggle for power, respect, and survival was a constant battle.

But as the years wore on, Marcus began to feel an emptiness inside. The thrill of the streets wasn't as fulfilling as it once was. It was a never-ending cycle of violence, betrayal, and the loss of people he loved. He began questioning his life, his purpose. One day, a fellow Crip—someone he had known for years but never really spoken to deeply— shared with him something that would change his path forever.

This guy, named Tyrell, had started reading the Bible. He wasn't some preacher or overly religious guy; he was just a man who found peace in what he'd been reading. He shared how he felt a deep connection with the ancient Israelites, believing that God had chosen the Israelites to be His people, just like Tyrell believed God had chosen him.

Marcus listened, intrigued.

After a few months of reading and studying the

Bible himself, Marcus made the decision to leave

his old life behind. He decided he was going to

become an Israelite. He embraced a new identity,

adopting a different mindset, and even started

calling himself by a Hebrew name he felt more

connected to. He felt good about it at first. The idea

of being part of a chosen people, of having a divine

purpose—this gave Marcus a sense of direction

and peace he hadn't known in years.

But things weren't as simple as he'd hoped. While

he found a new purpose in being an Israelite, the

struggles of his old life never fully disappeared.

Marcus still wrestled with **bitterness**—anger at the

world for what he had been through and the people who had hurt him. His family, too, didn't understand his newfound faith. His mother called him crazy for leaving the gang, and his cousins, who were still in the streets, mocked him for trying to "act holy." They saw him as the same old Marcus, just with a different title.

Then there was **the issue of family**. Marcus had a deep resentment toward his father for abandoning the family when he was a kid. His father was never there to teach him right from wrong, and now that he was trying to live a more righteous life, he couldn't forgive his father. Every time he saw his dad, the bitterness resurfaced, and the gap between them only seemed to grow.

And, there were still moments where Marcus faced the temptations of his old life—the draw of the streets, the sense of power and respect he once had. It was hard to let go of old habits, especially when those around him didn't respect the changes he was trying to make. There were days when he wanted to fall back into the comfort of the gang life, where things were familiar, and power was immediate.

Despite his deep desire to live according to the commandments of God, Marcus still struggled with truly following them. He would tell himself, "I'm chosen. I'm one of God's people," quoting verses from the Bible to justify his identity, but his actions didn't always align with the laws.

For example, Marcus knew about the **Ten Commandments**, especially the part about **not bearing false witness** and **honoring his parents**. Yet, he still found himself speaking ill of others—out of anger or frustration—and his bitterness toward his father meant he couldn't respect him as the Bible instructed.

He'd also hear teachings about **love** and **forgiveness** in the Bible, like when Jesus said, "Love your enemies, bless those who curse you" (Matthew 5:44), but it was hard to love those who had wronged him—especially the ones who had betrayed him in the streets.

And then there was **keeping the Sabbath** holy (Exodus 20:8). He understood it was a day of rest and worship, but on Sundays, he'd often end up caught in the cycle of life—running errands, hanging with the guys, or dealing with family issues. The rest he needed spiritually often felt out of reach because of everything else going on around him.

When things got tough, Marcus would often turn to the Bible for comfort. He'd find verses that spoke about Israel being God's chosen people—like Deuteronomy 7:6: "For you are a holy people to the

Lord your God; the Lord your God has chosen you to be a people for His treasured possession, out of all the peoples who are on the face of the earth." This made him feel justified in calling himself an Israelite. He felt a deep connection to this idea, believing that as a chosen individual, his identity was secure, no matter what.

But deep down, Marcus knew he wasn't fully living by the commandments. He wasn't following God's laws to the letter, and every time he did something that contradicted the teachings—whether it was holding on to bitterness, not forgiving his father, or falling back into old habits—he felt a gap between his identity as an Israelite and his actions.

Despite his struggles, Marcus's journey wasn't in vain. Over time, he started to understand that being an Israelite wasn't just about claiming an identity or quoting Bible verses when things were tough—it was about a deep transformation, about changing his heart and mind to align with the commandments and teachings he was learning.

The struggle to forgive, to deal with bitterness, to leave behind old ways of life—these weren't easy changes. But with time, prayer, and effort, Marcus began to see that living as God's chosen people wasn't about perfection. It was about striving, growing, and learning to live according to His will, even when it was hard. Slowly, he began working through his bitterness, forgiving his father, and

understanding that **following the commandments**

wasn't just about avoiding sin but also about

actively choosing love, justice, and holiness.

Marcus's story is a powerful reminder that choosing

to follow the path of the Israelites or adopting an

identity as God's people comes with challenges.

The Bible may give us guidance, but the journey to

fully living out its teachings requires personal

growth, change, and a willingness to confront the

struggles of life—bitterness, temptation, and even

family issues. Just as Marcus learned, it's not

about perfect adherence to the commandments

overnight. It's about the continual journey of

aligning your life with the values of the Bible,

seeking forgiveness, and living a life that reflects

your identity as G

god's chosen people. Let me break it down for you.

I've seen so many people today who identify as

descendants of Egyptian royalty, claiming

connections to the deities and the grandeur of

Egypt. But here's the thing—they forget the bigger

picture. They forget that Egypt was also the land

where their ancestors were slaves, caught in an

oppressive system, working under harsh

conditions, building an empire that wasn't theirs.

How can they claim royalty without recognizing the

painful truth of their history?

And then I see these same people preaching the truth from the Bible, talking about equality, justice, and freedom. But here's the kicker—they're wearing designer clothes underneath their robes, flaunting labels like they're something special. It's crazy! It's like they're trying to mix truth with the same old materialism, acting like they're above it all, yet living in the very system they claim to reject. They'll call themselves sons of God one moment, and then go back to cheating, lying, smoking, and fornicating, completely dismissing the word of the Most High. How can you claim to be living in truth, but not follow the truth in your actions?

The reality is this: if you're living in a system that promotes destruction and you don't want to be a part of it, you've got two choices: leave or conquer. But the truth is, the culture is so embedded in you that you'll complain about it while still playing the game. You can't blame the system when you're part of it, and you can't call yourself a king or a queen when you're still caught up in the chaos of the very thing you say you oppose. If you want to change, it starts with truly following the word of God, living the truth you preach, and stepping out of the system that holds you back.

You see, it's easy to talk about freedom, to talk about equality, to talk about being the chosen people, but the real question is: Are you living in the truth of those words? Or are you just stuck in a cycle, trying to look royal while still acting like a slave to a broken system?

It's not enough to just talk about the truth; you have to live it. If you're claiming to be a child of God, to be part of the chosen people, then your life should reflect that. The Bible isn't just a book of good ideas; it's a guide to how you should live—how you should treat others, how you should deal with your struggles, and how you should align your actions with the principles of the Most High. But when you choose to cheat, lie, and live in sin while wearing a facade of righteousness, you're only deceiving yourself.

If you're constantly complaining about the system that oppresses you, but you're still playing by its rules, then you're just another part of the machine. You can't call yourself free if you're still chained to the same habits, the same mindset, and the same destructive patterns. **True freedom** comes when you stand up and break free from all of it—when you align yourself with what the Bible teaches, not just when it's convenient or when it fits your narrative. You either rise above it, leave it, or you become part of it.

But here's the reality: it's easier to complain about being oppressed than it is to actually make the change. It's easier to claim power and authority over your life while staying stuck in a cycle of destruction than to face the discomfort of breaking those chains and living out the truth of who you're meant to be. The culture you've been brought up in, the mindset that has been instilled in you, makes it feel normal to keep living this way. But when you start questioning everything—when you start seeing how much of it doesn't line up with the principles of the Bible—you begin to see the truth. And it's up to you to decide whether to keep playing the role of the victim or to rise up and claim your true power.

You can't call yourself the "royal people" of Egypt while living under the same chains of slavery—whether it's slavery to sin, materialism, or a broken system. You can't expect to wear a crown when your life is full of contradictions. If you want to walk in the truth, you need to live by it every single day. Stop just talking about it and start living it. Stop using God's word as a justification for your bad choices. The Most High isn't looking for lip service; He's looking for obedience, for change, for real transformation in how you live your life.

So, if you're ready to walk the path of the Most High, you have to make the decision: Are you going to continue playing the game, wearing your purple robes and designer clothes while still living in sin? Or are you going to rise up, conquer, and live the truth you speak, following God's commandments with a heart and life that reflect His will? It's a choice only you can make, but it's the choice that will define your life.

You can't walk around the world in robes, acting like royalty, but still be bound by chains—chains that come in the form of hip-hop clothes, materialism, and false knowledge. You can talk big, claim you have wisdom and truth, but if you're living in contradiction, you're just part of a weak cult, pretending to have something that you don't. How can you speak of casting out demons or moving in power when you can't even speak your

native tongue or understand your own literature?

You can't just shout truth if you're living in error.

The reality is, people can see through the facade.

You might try to justify your actions by using hatred

and division to draw people in, but that's not power.

The truth is, even the government sees you're way

off, and they don't consider you a real threat

because there's no power behind your actions.

Real power is seen in unity—when people come

together with a shared vision and strength. But

when there's no substance behind what you're

saying, all the noise and talking mean nothing. A

whole lot of shouting with no power to back it up is just empty words.

Look, **military power** is real. **Praying with faith** and seeing results is real. **Building something that lasts**—whether it's a community, a business, or a movement—is real. But complaining? That's destructive. It gets you nowhere. If you're constantly complaining about the system you say you hate, but you still take money from that same system, it exposes the truth: you're part of it. You're not really rejecting it; you're just complaining without the will to change.

The bottom line is simple: stop complaining about a system you hate when you're benefiting from it. If you want change, stop talking and start doing. Real change comes through action, through power, through unity that actually means something. Otherwise, all you're doing is spinning your wheels, making noise, and getting nowhere. So, if you want to be more than just words, you need to live with purpose and strength. It's time to stop being a part of the problem and start being part of the solution.

If you want to walk in power, you need to stop faking it. You can't just claim to have a purpose, claim to be on a mission, but then stay stuck in a cycle of self-destruction, contradictions, and empty rhetoric. Real change doesn't happen when you're stuck in an echo chamber, shouting at the world but never doing the work to build something solid.

Power is about action, about sacrifice, about being consistent with your values. It's about standing up and putting in the work even when no one is watching. And if you don't have that kind of foundation, you're just pretending, and the world can see it.

True unity doesn't happen when people are divided by egos, by hatred, or by false claims of power. It happens when people come together with a common purpose, a clear understanding of who they are and what they stand for. It's about **strength in numbers**—not just getting people to join your movement, but getting them to act together in a way that builds and grows. A group of people walking in true unity is unstoppable. But a bunch of people who are lost in their own egos, who don't know their own history, their language, their purpose—that's not power, it's just noise.

You can't continue to talk about fighting back against the system, but then keep feeding into it by doing things that only reinforce the chains you say you want to break. If you're really about change, stop complaining and start building. If you hate the system, stop relying on it to get by. Real power comes from **self-sufficiency, discipline, and purpose**. It comes from knowing who you are and standing firm in that identity, no matter how uncomfortable it gets.

The real work is in how you live every day—not just in what you say or what you wear. If you want people to follow you, to see the truth, then you need to **live the truth**. Show them through your actions that you're not just part of the problem, but part of the solution. Lead by example. **Stop depending on the system** you say you hate. Build your own. Develop your own community. Raise your children with knowledge and understanding of who they are, their heritage, and their power.

Ultimately, it's about **strength**—real, lasting, unshakable strength. And strength doesn't come from complaining, from division, or from relying on a broken system. It comes from understanding your identity, your purpose, and your power. It comes from aligning your actions with your words, and living in a way that proves you have what it takes to lead and to conquer. If you're serious about this, it's time to make a change—stop talking about the problems and start working on the solutions. The world is watching, and it's time to show them what real power looks like.

If you're truly ready to see change, then you have to be willing to put in the hard work. It's easy to complain, easy to point fingers and say "this system is broken" or "we're oppressed," but the real power comes from knowing you have the ability to create a new system—one that reflects your true values and purpose. It's about **taking responsibility** for your life, your actions, and your community. **Leadership** isn't about being the loudest voice or wearing the most expensive clothes—it's about showing up every single day and doing the work.

Don't let your identity be defined by your circumstances or by the limitations of the system around you. The world is full of distractions, full of temptations that pull you away from your purpose. It's easy to get lost in the noise, to get distracted by wealth, fame, or material success, but none of that lasts. **True success** is about **lasting impact**—it's about building something that will stand the test of time. That's the kind of power we need.

You can't just claim to be about unity and justice if you're still allowing hate, division, and personal greed to rule your life. Real unity comes from understanding that we are all part of a larger purpose. And that purpose is bigger than just self-preservation or self-glorification—it's about elevating everyone around you. **True unity** is not just about gathering people around your ideas or your way of thinking, but about working together towards a common goal, even when it's difficult, even when it's uncomfortable.

If you really want to change the world, it starts with your own world. It starts with you being **consistent**, being **authentic**, and showing the world what it means to live with integrity, with discipline, and with real purpose. People will follow you, not because you have the most power or the biggest platform, but because they will see that you are genuinely living the principles you preach. They will see that you are about action—not just words.

It's time to stop relying on the system that you claim to hate. If you want to break free from it, then you have to start building something different. Stop expecting change to come from the outside. **Real change starts within**—within your own heart, your own mind, your own actions. Take responsibility for your life, your community, and your future. If you're serious about this, then stop complaining about the way things are and start working towards the way things should be.

Change isn't easy. Building power, creating something that will last, it requires sacrifice and hard work. But that's what true power is about. It's not about quick fixes, or about being loud or flashy. It's about consistent effort, faith, and dedication to your purpose. It's about being the kind of person who doesn't just talk the talk but walks the walk.

So, are you ready to stop being a part of the problem? Are you ready to step into your power, to create something better for yourself and your

community? Because that's what real leadership

looks like. **It's time to rise up. It's time to build.**

It's time to show the world the power of living

the truth.

This is where the truth hits home. The Bible calls

us a "peculiar people," and that's exactly what

we're meant to be. If you are the chosen people of

God, you are called to walk a different path—one

that isn't about blending in, isn't about following the

crowd, but about standing firm in your identity, your

purpose, and your faith. The sons of Judah—God's

people—are called to be a light, to walk in the

strength of the Most High, and to fight the battles that matter.

But here's the question: If you claim to be one of the chosen, if you claim to follow the Most High, then should you not know how to defeat the enemy? Shouldn't you have the ability to fight against the forces of darkness, to recognize and cast out demons, to break the chains that bind you? Or are you the type of person who talks big, who claims power and authority, but still can't overcome the strongholds in your own life? You might have a loud voice, but does your life reflect the power of that voice? Spiritual warfare is real, and it's not just a matter of saying words. It's about action. It's about recognizing the evil forces in this world and being equipped to fight them—whether those forces come in the form of demons, narcissism, mental health issues, or the broken systems that keep people trapped.

You can't claim to be walking in the light if you're still living in the darkness of sin, addiction, or confusion. Too many people are still struggling with strongholds—those mental and spiritual chains that keep you from being free. Whether it's addiction to substances, like smoking, or the bondage of bitterness, hatred, or unresolved trauma, if you're the chosen of God, then it's time to break free. The power is in you, but you have to access it. You have to be ready to fight back—not just with words, but with the truth and the authority that comes from knowing who you are in God.

Let's talk about the real story of the sons of Judah. This tribe, this bloodline, was here long before the colonizers came in and took over everything. They came, took what wasn't theirs, and tried to rewrite history. But the truth is, **the sons of Judah were here before anyone else**. The strength, the wisdom, the power—they are not new to the world. What happened? We became weaker, distracted by shiny things, by the promises of material wealth and false power. And in that weakness, we sold ourselves and each other out. We allowed others to come in and take what was rightfully ours. We allowed ourselves to be bound by things that didn't bring us life.

This is what spiritual warfare is about. It's about reclaiming what was taken. It's about standing in the truth of who we are, of who we were created to be. The battle isn't just physical—it's spiritual. And the sons of Judah, the chosen people of God, are called to be warriors. But not just warriors in the physical sense. We're called to be warriors in the spirit, to stand against the forces of darkness, to break down the strongholds, and to reclaim our inheritance.

The enemy is out here, trying to distract us with everything that glitter and glitters, while the real power is in knowing who we are and walking in that truth. You can't be someone who talks about being God's people but then let the chains of addiction, sin, or weakness hold you down. You can't be someone who prays and fasts, yet still lives in bondage. If you're truly the chosen of God, if you are part of that royal priesthood, then you have the power to defeat demons, to break the strongholds that have been placed on you, and to walk in freedom.

But that freedom comes through action. That freedom comes when you decide enough is enough. **Spiritual warfare is real**. Demons, strongholds, mental health issues—they are all real. And if you are the sons of Judah, you are called to fight. Not with just loud words, not with arrogance or pride, but with the authority that comes from walking in God's truth, from understanding the power of the Most High, and from living out that power every single day.

The time for talking is over. The time for action is now. Stand up, fight back, and reclaim what was always meant to be yours.

It's time to stop being complacent, stop being passive in the face of the battles that are happening right before our eyes. If you're truly a child of the Most High, you have been equipped with everything you need to overcome the darkness, to stand strong against the forces that are out to break you. You have to understand the weight of your heritage, the power within your bloodline. The sons of Judah were born to be warriors, to stand firm in truth, to bring light into the world. And yet, for too long, we've allowed ourselves to get distracted, sidetracked by false idols and empty promises. It's time to wake up and realize who we are.

When you look around today, it's clear that the world is in chaos. People are lost, trying to find peace in things that can never satisfy—material wealth, status, addictions, false teachings. And it's easy to get caught up in it all. But if you are truly the sons and daughters of Judah, you have been given the authority to fight back, to break those chains and walk in the freedom that was promised to you. **Spiritual warfare** is not just about fighting for your own soul—it's about fighting for the souls of your people, your family, and your community.

You can't continue to let the enemy hold sway over your life or your community. You can't continue to be enslaved by the chains of sin, addiction, or lack of knowledge. If you know who you are—if you know your identity in God—you are meant to stand firm and fight the darkness with the light that you carry. This is your battle. This is your responsibility.

The battle isn't just out there; it's within you.

You have to fight the temptation to stay in the comfort of your old ways, to stay quiet when you know the truth. You have to rise above the distractions and find the strength to stand in your identity as a child of God.

And if you're still battling with strongholds, with addiction, with anger, or with unforgiveness, don't think that just praying and fasting is enough if you're not ready to fight spiritually. Prayer and fasting are powerful tools, but they have to be backed by action. You need to go into battle armed with God's Word, armed with the knowledge of who you are, and you need to be ready to **speak life**, to **rebuke demons**, to **break strongholds** in your life and in the lives of those around you.

The power is in you. It's time to stop living in weakness, in confusion, or in fear. You are a royal priesthood, a chosen people, and it's time to start acting like it. The enemy knows who you are; it's time for you to know who you are. No more excuses. No more playing small. Stand up and take your rightful place in God's army.

The battle is real. The fight is hard. But you have everything you need to win. **God has equipped you with the tools to fight**. His Word is a sword, and your faith is a shield. Don't let the distractions of the world keep you from walking in your destiny.

Rise up, claim your power, and **fight for your people, your family, your community**. The Most High is with you, and if He is for you, who can stand against you?

You are more than a conqueror. **You are Judah—** a lion, strong and bold. Let's fight like it. Let's live like it.

I'm just an author, yes, a great one, and I love you all. Please, don't be mad at me for venting my truth. Use these words I'm sharing with you as a way to change the narrative. I remember a time when we, the chosen people, understood our purpose—we knew how to pray, we cleansed ourselves before entering the tabernacle of God,

we held the Ark of the Covenant with reverence.

But what practices do we hold now? It's all about

the swag, the material things, the outward

appearance. We've lost sight of the deeper

practices that once defined us.

At the end of the day, I love you, my brothers and

sisters. I'm not here to tear you down but to

challenge you to think, to awaken, to see what

we've become and how we can return to our true

purpose. We are so much more than the

distractions that surround us. Let this be a call to

open your eyes, to truly wake up and see the truth

that has been waiting for us to embrace it. We were

chosen for greatness, and it's time to reclaim that

greatness.

Open your eyes, brothers and sisters. It's time

for us to stand tall in the truth of who we are and

walk with purpose again.